BOSTON'S FREEDOM TRAIL

A Souvenir Guide

Sixth Edition

Illustrations by
Jack Frost

Text by
Robert Booth

Revised by
Erica Bollerud

The
Globe
Pequot
Press

GUILFORD, CONNECTICUT

Text design by Libby Kingsbury
Photographs and map appear courtesy of the Greater Boston
Convention and Visitors Bureau
Photo credit for page 28: Courtesy of Bostonian Society

Library of Congress Cataloging-in-Publication Data

Frost, Jack, 1915–
    Boston's Freedom Trail : a souvenir guide / illustrations by
Jack Frost ; text by Robert Booth.—6th ed. / revised by Erica
Bollerud.
        p. cm.
    Includes index.
    ISBN 0-7627-2665-2
        1. Historic sites—Massachusetts—Boston—Guidebooks. 2.
Freedom trail (Boston, Mass.)—Guidebooks. 3. Boston (Mass.)—
Guidebooks. 4. Boston (mass.)—History. I. Booth, Robert, II.
Bollerud, Erica. III. Title.

F73.7.F76 2003
917.44'61044—dc21   2003040804

Manufactured in the United States of America
Sixth Edition/First Printing

CONTENTS

FOREWORD

For 175 years the Freedom Trail in Boston was a concept without a name. In 1950 a Boston newspaperman, William G. Schofield, came to the realization that the greatest number of sites sacred to the beginnings of our Republic anywhere in the United States were located in Boston, and moreover they were all within easy walking distance of one another. Then, in a moment of inspiration, he conceived the name *Freedom Trail.*

Previously each site had its own organization and its individual idea of how to present itself to the public; as a result, the planning of an orderly visit was at best confusing, the less-than-studious visitor might easily go away having missed something significant. Now, as the Freedom Trail has brought all of these places together under the aegis of the Freedom Trail Foundation, it is easy for the visitor to get a rounded and balanced view of the historic sites and through such an experience to enhance his or her knowledge of American history. Most important, under the confederation that now exists, there is no compromise in the individuality with which each site is presented.

This has been worked out over a period of time, thanks to the efforts of many groups, including the Advertising Club of Boston, the Greater Boston Convention and Visitors Bureau, the Freedom Trail Commission, and, most recently, the National Park Service, which today plays a vital part in the maintenance and interpretation of the sites along the Trail.

This book is thus intended to present to the reader a package in which you will find admirably described each of Boston's significant historic places. We of the Freedom Trail Foundation welcome you to our city and trust that this booklet will help you make your visit both a memorable and an enjoyable experience.

—Charles F. Adams, former chairman of the Freedom Trail Foundation

FREEDOM TRAIL SITES AND STRUCTURES

The numbers on this page correspond with the numbers on the map on pages vi and vii.

1. Boston Common
2. State House, site of John Hancock's House
3. The Beacon
4. Park Street Church
5. Old Granary
6. King's Chapel and Burying Ground
7. Benjamin Franklin's Statue
8. The Old Corner Bookstore
9. Site of Franklin's Print Shop
10. Old South Meeting House
11. Site of Benjamin Franklin's Birthplace
12. Old State House
13. Site of the Boston Massacre
14. Faneuil Hall
15. Quincy Market
16. The Tea Party Ship
17. Paul Revere's House
18. Saint Stephen's Church
19. Paul Revere Mall
20. Old North Church
21. Copp's Hill
22. USS *Constitution*
23. Bunker Hill

(T) indicates entrance/exit for rapid transit stations. The name of the station appears next to the (T). The dotted line indicates the Freedom Trail walking tour.

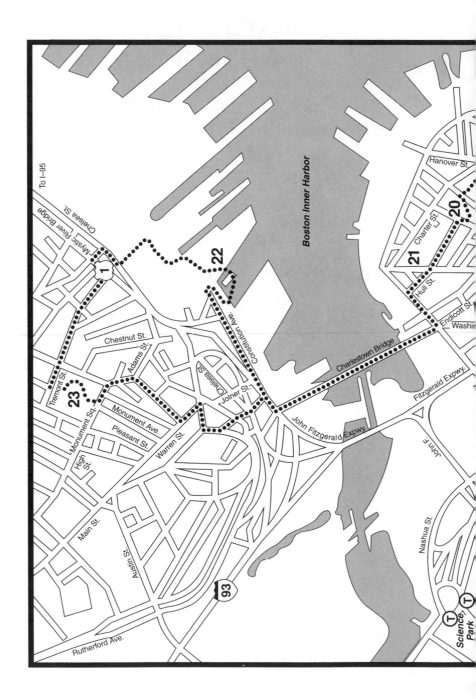

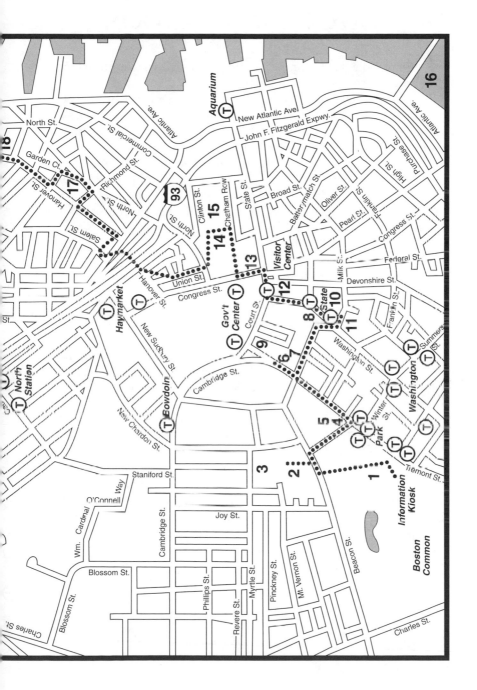

VISITOR INFORMATION

The Freedom Trail is one of the most popular walking tours in America. It covers approximately 3 miles and is easy to follow. The path is well marked by painted red lines or red bricks set into the pavement. Each site is identified by a distinctive marker or sign. Bear in mind that the Freedom Trail is a walking tour. Much of the Trail meanders through the twisting and curved streets that are the original paths and byways established by the first colonists. Do not attempt to drive the Trail. The best way to see everything is to walk. Many parts of the Trail are not accessible by car, bus, or any means of wheeled transportation except bicycle. This book includes the sixteen major sites, as well as important structures along the Trail.

You may pick up the trail anywhere along the route, but the most convenient and logical starting points are Boston Common and the USS *Constitution* in Charlestown, where parking is free.

Boston is equipped with an efficient public transportation system. Buses operate along the route of the Freedom Trail about every ten to fifteen minutes, seven days a week, generally from 6:00 A.M. to midnight. The Massachusetts Bay Transportation Authority's Web site at www.MBTA.com provides information about which station is nearest to each of the sites as well as schedules, routes, and fares. Information is also available by calling (617) 222–3200 Monday through Friday, 6:30 A.M. to 8:00 P.M., and weekends, 7:30 A.M. to 6:00 P.M.

Bus fare is 75 cents for adults and 35 cents for children five through eleven. Subway fare is $1.00 for adults and half price for children five through eleven. Children under five ride free. Visitor passes are available and cost $6.00 per person for one day, $11.00 per person for three consecutive days, and $22.00 per person for seven consecutive days.

Wheelchair travelers and persons sixty-five years of age or older may obtain reduced-fare passes from the Senior and Access Pass office by calling (617) 222–5976. To arrange for a lift bus, wheelchair travelers must call (800) LIFT–BUS (800–543–8287) by 1:00 P.M. at least one day in advance of travel. A message may be left twenty-four hours a day, detailing the route and the time of day travel is planned.

Many stations and the information booth on Boston Common provide free subway maps.

For further information, contact the Greater Boston Convention and Visitors Bureau at (888) SEE–BOSTON or bostonusa.com. You may also visit the following Web sites: www.cityofboston.gov; www.thefreedomtrail.org; www.nps.gov/bost.

The prices and rates listed in this guidebook were confirmed at press time. We recommend, however, that you call establishments to obtain current information before traveling.

BOSTON COMMON

*Bounded by Park, Tremont, Boylston, Charles,
& Beacon Streets*

There's nothing common about Boston Common, America's oldest public park.

John Winthrop, sometimes called "the American Moses," and his Puritan followers first pitched their tents here in 1630. The local Indians called the peninsula Shawmutt, meaning "living waters." The Puritans renamed the place Boston, after a town in England.

Their neighbor, the Reverend William Blackstone, already lived on the slope of Beacon Hill overlooking a pleasant expanse of meadow that ran down on its western side to the Back Bay, which in those days really was a bay. Rev. Blackstone, however, disliked having so much company, so, withholding six acres at the top of the hill, he sold his homestead to the town in 1634. Then he vanished into the wilderness. He reappeared in Boston twenty-five years later, riding a white bull and looking for a wife.

The Old England Puritans were accustomed to having "common land" reserved for such important public uses as pasturage for goats and cows, the pillory, and public executions, and a military parade ground for the local "trayn-band," or militia. In New England the common served similar purposes. Here William Robinson and Marmaduke Stevenson, convicted of being Quakers, were launched into eternity by hanging, and here Mary Dyer, Margaret Jones, and Mistress Anne Hibbins, proven consorts of His Satanic Majesty, were expunged from the Divine State. Here too, for unspecified crimes against the settlers in 1656, Matoonas, an Algonquian Indian sagamore, or subordinate chief, was tied to a tree and shot. These occasions were declared general holidays and attracted great crowds.

Before and during the early years of the Revolution, British regiments encamped on Boston Common. And in 1824, when General Lafayette made his goodwill trip to the young democracy, Boston's schoolchildren turned out on the Common to sing "La Marseillaise." The general was also honored by 1,200 people at a public banquet under a canopy on the Common.

Cows and sheep grazed on the Common until 1830, when they were banished. The Society for the Suppression of

1

The Robert Gould Shaw and Fifty-fourth Regiment Memorial

Intemperance convinced Mayor Harrison Gray Otis that he could "promote order and suppress an inclination to riot and intemperance" by holding municipal concerts on the Common. Ever since, music lovers have gathered in the shade of towering oaks for band concerts and crowded under moonlit skies for performances by popular entertainers. The Reverend Martin Luther King Jr., addressed thousands on the Common, and Pope John Paul II celebrated a public Mass there.

Boston Common provides a setting for many notable sculptures. The Soldiers and Sailors Monument, whose figures personify history and peace, rises like a vision from a hilltop. Brewer Fountain, just steps from the visitor's kiosk, debuted at the Paris Exposition in 1855, after which Gardner Brewer brought it to America for his Beacon Hill home. And the palette-shaped cenotaph just within the fence of the Central Burying Ground at the corner of Tremont and Boylston Streets honors painter Gilbert Stuart, who is buried in one of the unmarked graves.

Soldiers and Sailors Monument in Boston Common

The most famous sculpture is undoubtedly the Robert Gould Shaw and Fifty-fourth Regiment Memorial by Augustus Saint-Gaudens at the corner of Park and Beacon Streets, facing the State House. This bronze commemorates the bravery of the first black regiment to serve in the Civil War. Their colonel, the twenty-six-year-old Robert Gould Shaw, son of a prominent Boston family, and half of his regiment perished in the attack on Fort Wagner, South Carolina. A black butler, retired from service in the Shaw household, funded the memorial. The 1989 film *Glory* is a tribute to the regiment's heroism.

The long mall running from Beacon Street at the Joy Street entrance across the whole length of the Common to the corner of Boylston and Tremont Streets is called the Oliver Wendell Holmes Path. The eminent physician and writer recalled walking there with Amelia Lee Jackson: "I think I tried to speak twice without making myself distinctly audible. At last I got out the question—Will you take the long path with me?—Certainly,—said the schoolmistress,—with much pleasure—Think,—I said,—before you answer; if you take the long path with me now, I shall interpret it that we are to part no more. She answered softly, I will walk the long path with you!"

Walt Whitman and Ralph Waldo Emerson walked together for two hours on May 12, 1863, while the Sage of Concord used all of his powers of persuasion, without success, to convince Whitman to delete "The Children of Adam" portion of *Leaves of Grass*.

In the 1600s no one strolled the Common on Sunday, a day reserved for serious churchgoing. Nowadays Sunday is the Common's day to shine. Easter Sunday especially finds Boston families strutting their finery on the Common. And on warm summer days, strolling the Common offers relief from the city's parched pavement.

The Common is the first jewel in Frederick Law Olmsted's Emerald Necklace, 6 miles of greenery that encompasses the city. Office workers enjoy picnic lunches here. Retired folks relax on benches. Children splash in the Frog Pond in summer and ice-skate there in winter. And year-round people hand-feed friendly pigeons and squirrels.

Beneath the park's pastoral setting is a 1,365-car parking garage, and at the corner of Park and Tremont Streets is the entrance to the oldest subway in America. This corner has also been the site of memorable events, including the world's largest craps game, during the Boston police strike of 1919, and Vietnam War protests. Whatever the issue, soapbox orators provide entertaining street theater with their passionate commentary.

WEB SITE: *www.cityofboston.gov/freedomtrail /bostoncommon.asp*

SITE OF THE LIBERTY TREE

Washington and Essex Streets

A plaque on the building at the corner of Washington and Essex Streets marks the place where the Patriots' famed Liberty Tree stood.

The Liberty Tree played a pivotal role in the colonists' resistance to the Stamp Act, levied by the British Parliament in 1765 to help defray the cost of defending the American frontier. The Stamp Act taxed newspapers and various official and legal documents.

Boston was in an uproar. The colonists interpreted this tax as a flagrant example of taxation without representation and bitterly resented it. At daybreak on August 14, the birthday of the Prince of Wales, members of the Sons of Liberty hanged an effigy of Thomas Oliver from an elm tree in Hanover Square. Oliver was the Royal stamp collector and brother-in-law of the colony's lieutenant governor, Thomas Hutchinson.

During the day, word of the "hanging" spread, and soon thousands of people gathered at the spot to express their admiration and approval. At dusk the crowd took down the effigy, placed it on a funeral bier, and formed a vast torchlight procession to the stamp office, which they promptly tore apart.

After attacking the homes of various Royal officials, the mob built a bonfire and cremated the effigy. The next day the real Mr. Oliver was compelled to appear under the gallows of the Liberty Tree and to renounce his duties as a stamp officer.

5

A contemporary journalist reported, "After a long spell of laughing and grinning, sweating and swearing, and foaming with malice diabolical [British soldiers] cut down a tree because it bore the name of liberty." The patriots of Boston, however, renamed it the Liberty Stump and continued to use it as a place of assembly.

STATE HOUSE

Beacon and Park Streets

The State House, begun in 1795 and completed in 1798, is the crowning achievement of Charles Bulfinch, who also designed Connecticut's State House and was the architect for the Capitol in Washington, D.C.

After returning from an architectural tour abroad, Bulfinch submitted his design for the Massachusetts capitol in November 1787. He explained that it was "in the style of a building celebrated all over Europe," London's Somerset House on the banks of the Thames, a monumental neo-Palladian government building by Sir William Chambers. More than seven years elapsed before the design was implemented, however, and Samuel Adams and Paul Revere laid the cornerstone on July 4, 1795.

The State House originally was intended for a site on the lower part of the Common, but Bulfinch had begun to design and build handsome residences near John Hancock's mansion atop Beacon Hill, so the location was changed to this more fashionable part of town. For two and a half years, the architect supervised masons, carpenters, plasterers, carvers, painters, glaziers, and roofers, all of whom labored to create the finest public building in America. Progress was slow, expenses high; but when the State House was completed, it was an immediate success, praised as "the most magnificent building in the Union," a marvel of "perfect taste and proportion."

The original redbrick facade, now enlarged by two wings, generally resembles the pavilion of Lord Somerset's house; in detail, however, it is an original neoclassical Bulfinch composition. With blind-arched windows and elegant lunettes, the building—including flanking brick pavilions—is 173 feet across the front. Ninety-four feet of this expanse are occupied by the arched brick portico that supports a magnificent Corinthian

Gold dome of the State House

colonnade, which in turn is surmounted by a pilastered pediment.

The famous golden dome, 50 feet in diameter and 30 feet high, is a grand, dominating hemisphere. It is topped by a cupola and pinecone, symbol of the lumber industry and Maine, which at the time was part of Massachusetts. First painted lead gray, the dome was sheathed in copper in 1802 by Paul Revere and Sons. In 1861 it was gilded, and in 1874 gold-leafed. Except for a period during World War II when it was blacked out, the dome has gleamed for more than a century.

Enoch Williams, a nineteenth-century travel writer, reported on the view from the dome in his *Impressions of America* for London readers. "I speak soberly and without exaggeration," he wrote. "There are few views either in the new world or the old that can be compared to this."

The interior was just as handsome. Lofty ceilings, ornamental plasterwork by Daniel Raynard, and the richly carved columns and pilasters of the principal rooms were universally admired. Portraits of Massachusetts governors now hang in the entrance hall. The Sacred Cod, a 5-foot-long pinewood fish opposite the

speaker's desk in the Hall of Representatives, highlights the importance of the fishing industry in Massachusetts. Although the State House has been enlarged greatly and the interior extensively remodeled, the Bulfinch front remains intact, an authentic American temple to democracy.

After the State House was built, town fathers decided it would look more impressive without Boston's other hills around it. Mount Vernon, to the west, was used to fill the river and raise Charles Street. In 1845 Cotton Hill, on the east, was leveled and used to fill a millpond at its foot. This endeavor created eight acres of downtown land, including the site of the Court House.

By a twist of fate, the private fortune of Charles Bulfinch was sinking just as his public reputation reached its height. Committing nearly all of his wealth to an ambitious residential development known as the Tontine Crescent on Franklin Street, Bulfinch was unable to weather one of the many financial panics of the early Republic. In 1799, unwilling to see its great citizen reduced to

poverty, Boston elected him chief selectman and superintendent of police. As the town's leading administrator/architect, he improved nearly every aspect of his native place, from the execution of laws and the conduct of government to the planning and laying out of new streets and the design of dozens of residential, commercial, ecclesiastical, and institutional buildings.

Given Bulfinch's lifetime of extraordinary accomplishment, it is difficult to assign preeminence to any one of his projects; and yet the State House is regarded as Bulfinch's masterpiece. In one magnificent stroke he introduced a new architecture for the new nation, powerful and majestic, expressive of the ideals embodied in the Constitution of a self-governing people. America's first professional architect set a new standard and applied it to every aspect of Boston—a legacy of excellence that endures to this day.

HOURS: *9:00* A.M.–*5:00* P.M. *Monday–Friday, 10:00* A.M.–*4:00* P.M. *Saturday. Tours run 10:00* A.M.–*3:30* P.M. *Closed most state, federal, and legal holidays. Open Veterans Day, Columbus Day, Memorial Day.* ADMISSION: *Free*
TELEPHONE: *(617) 727–3676*
WEB SITES: *www.state.ma.us/sec/trs; www.cityofboston.gov/ freedomtrail/massachusettshouse.asp*
WHEELCHAIR ACCESSIBILITY: *Bowdoin Street*

SITE OF JOHN HANCOCK'S HOUSE

The house of John Hancock, which stood on what is now the west lawn of the State House, was torn down in 1863. One of the last of the great Georgian mansions in Boston, as notable architecturally as it was historically, it was built in 1737 for John's uncle Thomas Hancock, a wealthy merchant who had started out as a bookbinder and stationer.

Two stories high and constructed of Connecticut stone brought to Boston by boat, the mansion boasted a gambrel roof, corner quoins, four large chimneys, an elegant rooftop captain's walk, and a richly paneled interior—all in all, the house of an English squire. For thirty years, until painter John Singleton Copley built his mansion, the Hancock house stood in solitary splendor among formal gardens and fruit trees on the side of old Beacon Hill, overlooking the green expanse of the Common. On Thomas's death in 1764, the estate passed to his widow. When she died in 1777, she left it to her favorite nephew, a high-living young dandy who was just beginning to espouse the cause of liberty.

Having inherited a fortune—particularly helpful to someone who was not adept at commerce—John Hancock plunged into the revolutionary politics of the day. He served as moderator of the Boston town meeting, sat as a member of the town's various rebel committees, and later became president of both the Massachusetts Revolutionary Congress and the Continental Congress in Philadelphia.

British soldiers occupied the house at the time of the signing of the Declaration of Independence, a fact that some suggest accounts for the boldness of Hancock's signature. George III had put a price on Hancock's head. When Hancock became the first signer of the Declaration of Independence, he rendered his autograph with a conspicuous flourish and declared, "John Bull can read that without spectacles! Now let him double his reward!"

Hancock served as first governor of Massachusetts, and at the end of his life he attempted to donate his house to the Commonwealth for a museum of the Revolution or a governor's mansion. The Commonwealth declined. Even after his heirs persisted, the gift was refused, and so the house was torn down.

THE BEACON

Behind the State House

Beacon Monument, facing Ashburton Place, marks the highest point in the city. When the first settlers arrived, Boston had three hills. On Sentry Hill, the highest, settlers erected a tall pole with rungs all the way up for a man to climb. On top of this lookout, they filled a pot with pitch and pinewood. In times of danger—fire or attack by Indians or the British—they set a fire to warn the inhabitants of the town. Thus the name Beacon Hill.

During the years of rebellion, the beacon blazed frequently. When the old structure blew down in 1789, the site therefore

The Beacon

seemed appropriate for a monument "to commemorate the train of events which led to the American Revolution."

Charles Bulfinch designed Boston's first Revolutionary War monument, which was erected in 1791 to the acclaim of the city. Of stuccoed brick and stone, the 60-foot-high memorial column was topped with an eagle. In 1811, however, Beacon Hill's crest was removed for landfill; the column came down. A copy of the monument, incorporating its original tablets, was built in 1865 on the present site, where Bulfinch's vigilant eagle proudly stands guard.

PARK STREET CHURCH

Corner of Tremont and Park Streets

The elegant Park Street Church, erected in 1809, dominates its streetscape; it is a masterpiece of ecclesiastical architecture and, according to Henry James, "the most interesting mass of brick and mortar in America."

The church stands on the site once occupied by Boston's Old Granary, a huge barn that became so infested with rats and weevils that the town sold it. New owners cleaned out both the grain and the vermin and used the building for commercial purposes, including a sail loft where "Old Ironsides's" first sails were stitched. When the Old Granary was finally torn down, frugal Yankees recycled its timbers to build a tavern.

Peter Banner, the church's English architect, had recently arrived in Boston from Connecticut, where he had designed buildings for Yale University. Banner drew on nearly every element of Charles Bulfinch's residential design vocabulary, infused it with the grace of Sir Christopher Wren's London spires, and produced an edifice so striking and so enduring that the Trinitarian Evangelical congregation has never left.

Although the lofty steeple was shortened after a bad spell of swaying in the nineteenth century, Park Street Church still presents an extremely graceful facade, with bowfront colonnades, a Palladian tower window, recessed arches, a pedimented belfry, a towering steeple, and carved wood detail by Boston's Solomon Willard, architect of the Bunker Hill Monument. To these classic elements Banner added one unusual feature: semicircular porches between the tower base and the body of the main building.

Park Street Church

Park Street Church

Despite its superior commercial site in the heart of downtown Boston, the church has never been endangered by possible sale or demolition. During a period of financial difficulty, however, part of the building was rented out as a tearoom, until it was discovered that women were displeasing the Lord by smoking cigarettes.

Still, its downtown location brought risk. On a Sunday morning in November 1895, as the pastor sat in his study working on a sermon, the windows suddenly came crashing in, and the clergyman found himself fighting for his life in an avalanche of mud. He escaped, but, along with his evening sermon, the study was ruined.

Investigation revealed that a workman, digging a nearby tunnel for America's first subway, had broken a huge water main. That evening the minister delivered a sermon filled with righteous wrath, denouncing the subway as "an infernal hole" and suggesting that none other than Satan had been responsible for the "unchristian outrage."

16

Park Street Church is forever associated with fiery sermons. On the Fourth of July 1829, William Lloyd Garrison, the great abolitionist and publisher of the *Liberator*, gave his first public antislavery address—an oration not well received by his audience, who at one point tried to lynch him. And in 1849 Senator Charles Sumner delivered his powerful oration, "The War System of Nations," to the American Peace Society.

In part as recognition of the many hellfire-and-brimstone sermons thundered from its pulpit, and in part because brimstone was stored in the church's cellar during the War of 1812, the corner of Park and Tremont Streets is known as Brimstone Corner.

The first Sunday school was organized at Park Street Church in 1817, and the first missionaries to Hawaii were dispatched from this church.

On Independence Day 1832 Samuel Francis Smith's song "America," also known as "My Country 'Tis of Thee," was first sung here.

HOURS: *July and August only, Tuesday–Saturday, 9:30* A.M.*–3:30* P.M.
Winter hours by appointment only.
Sunday services are held year-round at 8:30 A.M., *11:00* A.M., *4:00* P.M., *and 6:00* P.M.
ADMISSION: *Free*
TELEPHONE: *(617) 523-3383*
WEB SITE: *www.cityofboston.gov/freedomtrail/parkstreet.asp*
WHEELCHAIR ACCESSIBILITY: *Yes*

OLD GRANARY

Tremont Street, Near Park Street Church

The Old Granary Burying Ground was laid out in 1660 as the Old South Burying Ground on land that was part of Boston Common.

"There is a lovely solemnity about this little cemetery," noted Eleanor Early in her 1930 book, *This Is Boston*. "For nearly three hundred years it has kept its hallowed peace. Its headstones are little and dull, and covered with moss. And the trees that shelter them are grim and old. And, after dark, the little night winds sob as they tiptoe through the gloom."

The cemetery takes its name from an ugly wooden building erected in 1737 to store wheat and other grains for distribution to the poor. The granary stood between the graveyard (where pigs were allowed to browse) and the rest of the Common (where cows were turned out to graze). In 1738, one door up from the cemetery, the town built its workhouse to feed the indigent, who were forced to work. This Puritan tryptich—repositories for the staff of life, failed hopes and hard labor, and triumphant death—created a stark moral streetscape.

Since 1809 the beautiful Park Street Church has occupied the site of the granary and the workhouse. Its lithe lines contrast with the heavily symbolic granite gate of the Old Granary Burying Ground, decked with a winged globe and downturned torches.

More than 1,600 graves are in the Old Granary Burying Ground, sometimes called the Westminster Abbey of the nation. In addition to ordinary men, women, and children who pioneered the little world of Boston, scores of Revolutionary War soldiers, the city's first mayor, John Phillips, and the five Boston Massacre victims are buried here. This is also the final resting place of three signers of the Declaration of Independence—John Hancock, Samuel Adams, and Robert Treat Paine—along with eight governors; philanthropist Peter Faneuil, "Funel" on his flat stone; diarist Judge Samuel Sewall, who lived to repent his part in the witchcraft trials; Paul Revere; and Benjamin Franklin's parents, whose grave is marked with its original stone and an obelisk erected in 1827 by the citizens of Boston.

Among old graveyards with their illustrious dead, their quaint inscriptions, and above all their sense of repose, Old Granary is

Franklin Obelisk

unsurpassed. Many seventeenth-century stones still stand, richly lettered and carved with ghastly death's heads and emblems of the fruits of paradise, Puritan symbols of the departing soul and the blissful eternity that is its destination. The oldest marker in the cemetery belongs to Hannah Allen; the oldest upright stone, to John Wakefield. Among other markers is the 1690 stone of Mary Goose, who, although a mother, was not Mother Goose. That literary distinction belongs to the second wife of Isaac Goose, Elizabeth, who had charge of so many children (twenty) that it is perfectly possible she did not know what to do.

The burying ground harbors some lesser-known but interesting characters, too. Ann Pollard, a child when she arrived with the first settlers, was the first to hop ashore at Shawmutt, later known as Boston. She grew up, married, and gave birth to numerous children. Surviving her husband by decades, she followed an independent, pipe-smoking course and operated the wild-and-woolly Horse Shoe Tavern. At the age of 103, she had her portrait painted. When she died two years later, the whole town joined her hundred-plus descendants in mourning her.

Benjamin Woodbridge found his way into this resting place in 1728. He made an injudicious remark at the Royal Exchange, the merchants' gathering place, and was challenged to a duel with swords. He accepted. The affair of honor, held on Boston Common, ended with a rapier running through the twenty-year-old.

The story of Elisha Brown is etched on his stone. During the British occupation of Boston, he single-handedly prevented an entire regiment of His Majesty's troops from dispossessing him of his spacious home, which they coveted as a barracks. Years later he died a peaceful death in that home.

HOURS: *Daily, 9:00 A.M. to 5:00 P.M.*
ADMISSION: *Free*
TELEPHONE: *Boston Parks Department,*
(617) 635–4505
WEB SITES: *www.nps.gov/bost/Granary_Burying–Ground.html; www.cityofboston.gov/freedomtrail/parkstreet.asp*
WHEELCHAIR ACCESSIBILITY: *Limited; four steps to enter in front, but gate at rear (off Beacon Street) has ramp.*

KING'S CHAPEL

58 Tremont Street

In 1688, after townsfolk refused to sell him land, the despotic Royal Governor, Sir Edmund Andros, appropriated a corner of the Puritan town's first graveyard for a small wood chapel, complete with spire, to house the first Anglican congregation in North America.

Sentiment against Andros had been building, and this affront provoked such strong hostility from the colonists that he was forced to flee. But King's Chapel remained. Royal officials continued to worship in handsome style, surrounded by opulent decoration. Before the church was built, William and Mary had presented the communion table and chancel tables, still in use. Dukes and earls donated silver service. Queen Anne and King George III also favored the church with gifts of silver and vestments.

The congregation grew, and in 1710 the building was enlarged. By 1741 Boston's Anglicans had decided to replace the old wood chapel with a London-style stone edifice, but the project was deferred until 1748, when funds were raised. The congregation retained the talents of Peter Harrison, a gentleman designer from Newport, Rhode Island. Harrison's final design called for a substantial stone building and tower, to be lightened by the "beautiful effect" of a lofty wood steeple. He also proposed a double row of windows, the lower smaller than the upper, causing one wit to comment that he "had heard of the Cannons of the Church, but had never before seen the portholes."

When Governor William Shirley laid the cornerstone for the new edifice in August 1749, angry Puritans threw garbage. Nevertheless, great blocks of rough-hewn stone walls soon rose around the chapel, which was used until 1753. Then it was demolished and thrown out the windows of its successor.

Because money ran out, the "beautiful effect" of Peter Harrison's steeple was never realized. Yet the interior of the new church was a marvel of Georgian elegance and home to New England's first church organ. When the building was completed in 1754, the Anglicans were well pleased.

During the siege of Boston, British military and naval officers worshipped here. With the hasty departure of the Tories,

King's Chapel

The Wheelbarrow Walk next to King's Chapel

Boston removed the *King* from the chapel and rechristened it Stone Chapel. The name didn't last.

In 1790, shortly after George Washington attended an oratorio, the colonnaded portico was added. (The Ionic columns look like granite but are actually wood.) The final change took place in 1785, when the first Episcopal church in New England became the first Unitarian church in America. The congregation, however, summoned by Paul Revere's bell, still uses the Anglican *Book of Common Prayer.*

HOURS: *Columbus Day to Patriot's Day (third Monday in April), Saturday, 10:00* A.M.–*2:00* P.M.; *Patriot's Day to mid–June, Monday, Friday, and Saturday, 10:00* A.M.–*2:00* P.M., *occasionally Sunday, 1:00–3:00* P.M.; *mid–June to Labor Day, Monday, Friday, and Saturday, 9:30* A.M.–*4:00* P.M., *Tuesday and Wednesday, 9:30–11:00* A.M., *usually Sunday 1:00–3:00* P.M.; *Labor Day to Columbus Day, Monday, Friday, and Saturday, 10:00* A.M.–*2:00* P.M., *occasionally Sunday, 1:00–3:00* P.M.
Special guided tours are available with one day's notice. Call (617) 523–1749 or 227–3155.

23

ADMISSION: *Suggested donation $1.00 for adults*
TELEPHONE: *(617) 523–1749*
WEB SITE: *www.cityofboston.gov/freedomtrail/kingschapel.asp*
WHEELCHAIR ACCESSIBILITY: *Main floor of church partly accessible*

KING'S CHAPEL BURYING GROUND

Tremont Street

For thirty years this was the town's only burying ground. In September 1630 Sir Isaac Johnson, a leader of the Massachusetts Bay Company, succumbed to the rigors of the New World and was buried in the southwest corner of his garden lot. As other Puritans planned for their demise, they asked to be buried alongside Brother Johnson.

King's Chapel Burying Ground is the final resting place of nearly the entire first generation of Boston's English settlers. The oldest gravestone in Boston, William Paddy's 1658 marker, is found here. The Massachusetts Bay Colony's first governor, John Winthrop; William Dawes, who accompanied Paul Revere on his midnight ride; architect Charles Bulfinch; and Elizabeth Pain, the model for Nathaniel Hawthorne's Hester Prynne in *The Scarlet Letter*, are interred here, too. Mary Chilton, who arrived with the Pilgrims on the *Mayflower* and was the first Englishwoman to set foot in New England, is here, too, as are the pastors of the First Church and other early notables. After the Episcopal church was erected on the corner, Royal Governor William Shirley and other Tory officials, along with British soldiers, were interred here, as well.

The present arrangement of the headstones is the work of an old-time superintendent of burials. He apparently considered the beautifully carved old slates to be elements of a composition (his), rather than accurate grave markers. Perhaps this is why the old First Graveyard, or King's Chapel Burying Ground, is replete with legends of ghostly doings and supernatural restlessness.

The most famous ghost story is told of the notorious pirate Captain Kidd. According to legend, Captain Kidd was once such a respected citizen that the colonial governor commissioned him to apprehend pirates. Kidd stayed away for years, however, and people became suspicious. It was rumored that he had captured several ships and kept their stolen treasure: 1,111 ounces of gold, 2,353 ounces of silver, 57 bags of sugar, and 41 bales of other goods.

England ordered Captain Kidd's arrest. In 1700 he was taken prisoner and held in a Boston jail before being sent to London, where he was tried and hanged. No one is quite sure how his body came to be buried at King's Chapel Burying Ground. According to this tale, however, if you go to the cemetery at midnight, tap three times on a big gray stone, and whisper into the dark, "Captain Kidd, for what were you hanged?" Captain Kidd will answer—nothing.

HOURS: *Daily, 8:00* A.M.–*5:00* P.M.
ADMISSION: *Free*
TELEPHONE: *Boston Parks Department,*
(617) 635–4505
WEB SITE: *www.cityofboston.gov/freedomtrail/*
kingschapel.asp
WHEELCHAIR ACCESSIBILITY: *Yes*

BENJAMIN FRANKLIN'S STATUE

Old City Hall Grounds, 45 School Street

Erected in 1856, this 8-foot-tall bronze likeness of Benjamin Franklin by Richard S. Greenough is Boston's first public portrait statue. In executing the commission, the sculptor observed that he "found the left of the great man's face philosophical and reflective, and the right side funny and smiling." Tablets on the base recall scenes from Franklin's life.

The statue is located in front of Boston's Old City Hall, an ornate edifice built in 1862 in the French Second Empire style, which seems particularly appropriate since Franklin served as this country's first ambassador to France.

On the sidewalk in front of the statue, *City Carpet,* a mosaic by Lilli Ann Killen Rosenberg, marks the original site of Boston Latin School, the first public school in America. Brass letters, Venetian glass, and ceramic pieces spell out the names of its famous alumni, including Samuel Adams, Cotton Mather, and John Hancock. Franklin received his few years of formal schooling and a taste for books at Boston Latin School, sometimes called the Free Writing

25

BENJAMIN FRANKLIN
BORN IN BOSTON, 17 JANUARY 1706.
DIED IN PHILADELPHIA 17 APRIL, 1790

School, which opened in 1635 and established a standard of excellence that continues at its home on Avenue Louis Pasteur.

Largely self-taught, Franklin excelled as a printer, writer, editor, inventor, scientist, military officer, politician, and statesman. He is the only American who signed all four of the critical documents in Revolutionary-era history: the Declaration of Independence, the Treaty of Alliance with France, the treaty of peace with Great Britain, and the Constitution of the United States

WEB SITES: *www.nps.gov/bost/Ben_Franklin_Statue. htm; www.cityofboston.gov/freedomtrail/firstpublic.asp*

THE OLD CORNER BOOKSTORE

3 School Street, Corner of Washington Street

In 1712, a year after fire had destroyed the neighborhood, Thomas Crease built this solid brick house as his residence and Boston's first apothecary shop. With its steep gambrel roof, brick belt courses, and corner quoins, the English-style townhouse was one of the handsomest in the community of about 10,000 people.

Almost a hundred years earlier, the land belonged to William Hutchinson. Hutchinson's brilliant wife, Anne, ministered to the sick and held informal discussion groups for women in her home. Her controversial religious teachings challenged the male clergy and led to a dangerous Puritan schism, so in 1634 the General Court (the Massachusetts legislature) banished her from the colony. Anne Hutchinson took her husband and fourteen children first to Rhode Island with Roger Williams, then to Pelham, New York, where, except for one daughter, all were killed by Indians.

The Crease house became a bookshop in the 1820s, when the building was acquired by William D. Ticknor. A resourceful young man, he obtained the rights to publish works of British authors by adopting the then novel practice of paying royalties. In 1833 Ticknor took in as partner James T. Fields, a book clerk who astonished his colleagues by correctly predicting, as soon as they entered the shop, what books customers would buy.

Fields was instrumental in helping the company to sign contracts

The Old Corner Bookstore

with New England authors, and from 1833 to 1864 Ticknor and
Fields, Inc. was the country's leading publisher. Its authors
included Henry Wadsworth Longfellow, Harriet Beecher Stowe,
Nathaniel Hawthorne, Ralph Waldo Emerson, John Greenleaf
Whittier, Oliver Wendell Holmes, and Henry David Thoreau.
Walden and "The Battle Hymn of the Republic" were published
here.

In this Golden Age of American Literature, the publisher's
office/bookstore was the country's literary heart, an informal
clubhouse where writers could always find good conversation and
a glass of claret. Here, too, the famous Saturday Club was born.
Its members were the backbone of the house magazine, the
Atlantic Monthly. James Fields was the magazine's second editor.

After Ticknor and Fields moved out, the building housed a number of different booksellers. By the mid-twentieth century, it had

become a pizza parlor in a prime location for a new parking garage. With encouragement from the city and financial assistance from the Boston Globe Newspaper Company, Historic Boston, Inc., purchased the building in 1960 and restored it to its original appearance.

The Old Corner Bookstore, Inc., operated a branch of the Globe Corner Bookstore at this site until 1997; it now has stores in Back Bay and Harvard Square. Today, Historic Boston conducts its citywide preservation efforts in upstairs office space. On the ground floor, the Boston Globe Store perpetuates the tradition of using this site for the exchange of ideas through commerce. Here visitors can browse through guidebooks, posters, and regional memorabilia in a retail store where history was made in the early days of the nation.

HOURS: *Monday–Friday, 9:00* A.M.*–6:00* P.M.; *Saturday, 9:30* A.M.*–5:00* P.M.*; Sunday, 11:00* A.M.*–4:00* P.M.
ADMISSION: *Free*
TELEPHONE: *(617) 367–4000*
WEB SITES: *www.cityofboston.gov/freedomtrail/oldcorner.asp; www.nps.gov/bost/Old_Corner_Bookstore.htm*
WHEELCHAIR ACCESSIBILITY: *On first floor*

SITE OF FRANKLIN'S PRINT SHOP

Court Street

A bronze tablet on the Franklin Street facade of the building at 17 Court Street marks the place where Benjamin Franklin was apprenticed to his brother. James had gone to London to learn "the art or mystery" of printing, a rare calling in New England. Upon his return, he established a print shop and, in 1721, launched a newspaper, the *New-England Courant*.

James Franklin was a good printer, and, as a newspaperman, he possessed a sure sense of what his readers wanted to know. Young Ben's sprightly writing under the byline "Mrs. Silence Dogood" also contributed to the paper's success. Indeed the *New-England Courant* soon put the competition, the *Boston News-Letter,* out of business.

Ben set the type by hand; absorbed the literary and political

Artist's rendering of what Franklin's print shop may have looked like

influences of the newspaper office and pressroom; and printed books, broadsides, and circulars, all of which he hawked on the street. He obtained the best informal education a hardworking printer's devil could hope for.

"In a little time," he wrote, "I made great proficiency in the business, and became a useful hand." In addition to his duties as typesetter, pressman, and newsboy, young Ben wrote some topical verse that was published in broadside form.

James's ability to reflect his townspeople's real interests and opinions, however, gave offense to the conservative legislature, the Massachusetts General Court, which imprisoned him for a month. Ben ran the newspaper during his brother's absence and continued, as he put it, "to give our rulers some rubs in it." After James was released with the injunction he not print the *Courant*, the paper was published in Benjamin's name.

Eventually, the brothers had a falling-out. James was an abusive brother and master. Ben bitterly resented him and later wrote, "His harsh and tyrannical treatment of me [was] a means of impressing me with that aversion to arbitrary power that has stuck to me thro' my whole life."

Armed with a love of politics and of writing, the self-reliant seventeen-year-old secured a release from his indenture and booked passage on a boat bound for Philadelphia. From Philadelphia, Ben traveled to London, where he published his "Dissertation on Liberty and Necessity, Pleasure and Pain." By 1726 he was back in Philadelphia, writing tracts and publishing his own newspaper. In 1732, he began the witty and worldly *Poor Richard's Almanac*, which helped to define the newly emerging American character: industrious, practical, and optimistic.

Travelers who have experienced unwelcome interrogation by strangers can appreciate the impatience of the peripatetic Franklin. Weary of nosy tavern keepers who pumped guests for the latest news, he cut off their attempts at conversation with a set response. "My name is Benjamin Franklin," he would say. "I was born in Boston. I am a printer by profession and am traveling to Philadelphia. I shall have to return at such and such a time, and I have no news. Now what can you give me for dinner?"

Although Franklin is associated with his adopted state of Pennsylvania, Massachusetts proudly claims him as a native son. In 1778, the Commonwealth named a town in honor of the statesman, scholar, and humanist. To show his appreciation, Franklin considered giving his namesake either a church bell or a collection of books. Finally, he decided on books. His reason, he said, was that "sense [is] more essential than sound."

OLD SOUTH MEETING HOUSE

310 Washington Street, Corner of Milk Street

The Old South Meeting House stands on the site of the Puritans' original meetinghouse, a place of worship built in 1669 for dissenters from the First Church. They had sought a more liberal policy for church membership, and the first meeting house was a typical Puritan structure, severe in its lines and devoid of a steeple or anything else that might give the appearance of a church.

To the Puritans a church was a building in which the rites of the Church of England were observed. They had broken from that

Old South Meeting House

church and its "popish" liturgy. In their eyes a plain, barnlike meetinghouse was as acceptable to God as any cathedral in Christendom.

Two generations of prosperity and theological evolution, and a by then fashionable congregation, resulted in a new house of worship being built in the latest style. The Third Religious Society razed the old building in 1729. In its place they erected the present Georgian structure with brick laid in Flemish bond.

Josiah Blanchard's massive building features Palladian windows, a tower, a 180-foot wooden steeple, a belfry, and a two-tier gallery. Negro slaves—including Phillis Wheatley, America's first black woman author—sat in the topmost tier of the gallery. Although the congregation persisted in calling it a meetinghouse, the building was and is unmistakably a church, Boston's second oldest, and a model for much colonial ecclesiastical architecture.

By the middle of the eighteenth century, Boston, a prosperous English city, had a population of 25,000. In these years Old South was frequently used for mass gatherings and town meetings too large to fit into Faneuil Hall. The largest and most famous assembly occurred on the afternoon of December 16, 1773, when thousands of people crowded into the meeting house and thronged the streets outside to hear Sam Adams orate on the nonimportation of certain British goods, particularly those to be found in the holds of three recently arrived merchant vessels.

After Adams, Josiah Quincy spoke. He recognized in the meeting attendants' outrage and the governor's intransigence the makings of a mighty tempest. "I see the clouds which now rise thick and fast upon the horizon," Quincy declared. "The thunders roll and the lightnings play, and to the God who rides on the whirlwind and directs the storm I commit my country!" The crowd responded with a mighty whoop, and off it surged, torches blazing, to the waterfront for an evening tea party.

On another evening Dr. Joseph Warren, the handsome, aristocratic physician who died at Bunker Hill, was prevented from entering Old South. Not to be deterred, the young rebel climbed over the heads of British soldiers, through a second-story window in back, and addressed the patriots inside. His daring so humiliated the British that he became a marked man.

Right up to the outbreak of the Revolution, Old South served as a rebel auditorium as well as a place of worship. Because no other structure in Boston was so readily identified with the patriotic cause, the British took special revenge here.

33

Old South Meeting House

From June 1774 to June 1776, the years during which the Red-coats occupied Boston, Old South was used as an officers' club and a riding academy, with a liquor dispensary in the gallery. The pulpit was torn down; the high box floor was broken up for kindling. In the large open area thus created, several tons of dirt were dumped and raked smooth. Where the word of God and of man had rung out, the Queen's Light Dragoons spurred their mounts round and round, sometimes to drunken applause from the gallery above.

After the British were expelled from Boston, the congregation returned to its meetinghouse and restored the interior to its former state, including candlelight chandeliers and a white pulpit. The people of the town continued to hold overflow meetings here. The only lasting effect of the British presence was the loss of many valuable documents, including the manuscript of Pilgrim Governor William Bradford's *History of Plymouth*. Some fifty years later, however, the priceless documents were accidentally discovered in England. A letter from George Washington to his dentist, thanking him for a set of artificial teeth, was returned and is kept in Old South's safe.

Twice Old South has nearly gone up in smoke. In December 1810 the roof caught fire, and the building seemed doomed. Fortunately, the efforts of a courageous mastmaker, Isaac Harris, proved equal to the task. In gratitude for his extraordinary rooftop exertions, the Third Religious Society presented him with an elegant silver water pitcher, which is now on display in the Museum of Fine Arts.

Old South was threatened again in 1872, when the greatest of all the city's fires destroyed sixty-five acres of downtown Boston. Only judicious dynamiting of nearby structures halted the conflagration just short of Old South. Afterward Old South was pressed into service in a new role, as a temporary post office.

Preserved from the ravages of fire, the Old South Meeting House soon faced demolition in the name of progress. After bitter debate in 1875, the congregation built a new Old South in the Back Bay and put its former home up for sale.

The noble old building, located on a valuable commercial site, seemed destined for the wrecker's ball. Boston authors Ralph Waldo Emerson, Julia Ward Howe, and Louisa May Alcott successfully campaigned to stop the demolition. In a remarkable burst of civic pride, Bostonians formed an Old South Association. In short order they raised the $400,000 purchase price—the first instance of urban historical preservation in America.

The association continues to maintain Old South as a museum. Its venerable walls reverberate with the sounds of meetings, lectures, plays, concerts, memorial services, and church services. It is a living monument to the days and deeds of Otis, Adams, Quincy, and others who forged a new nation.

HOURS: *April 1–October 31, 9:30* A.M.*–5:00* P.M.; *November 1–March 31, 10:00* A.M.*–4:00* P.M.; *Closed Thanksgiving, Christmas Eve, Christmas Day, New Year's Day.*
ADMISSION: *Adults, $5.00; senior citizens and students, $4.00; ages six–eighteen, $1.00*
TELEPHONE: *(617) 482–6439*
WEB SITES: *www.oldsouthmeetinghouse.org; www.nps.gov/bost/ OSMH.htm; www.cityofboston.gov/freedomtrail/oldsouth.asp*
WHEELCHAIR ACCESSIBILITY: *Yes*

SITE OF BENJAMIN FRANKLIN'S BIRTHPLACE

17 Milk Street

A bronze plaque and a bust of Ben Franklin on the second story at 17 Milk Street, the Boston Post Building, commemorate the site where Franklin was born on January 17, 1706. This building now houses the Dreams of Freedom exhibit, which tells the story of Boston as America's second largest immigration gateway.

His father, Josiah Franklin, an English dyer, arrived in Boston in 1682. After the death of his first wife, Josiah married Abiah Foulger of Nantucket and entered into the messy and malodorous business of soap boiling. He was a tallow chandler, or maker and seller of candles.

In 1691 the elder Franklin had a family home built on Milk Street. His youngest son, the fifteenth of his seventeen children, was born here and christened Benjamin Franklin.

Fire destroyed the modest wood-frame house in 1810.

OLD STATE HOUSE

206 Washington Street

The Old State House, built in 1713, is the oldest surviving public building in Boston. It served as the capitol of the colonial British government before becoming home to the Massachusetts Assembly, the most radical of the colonial legislatures, and was the setting for George Washington's triumphal 1789 return to Boston, as well as for the inauguration of the Commonwealth of Massachusetts's first governor, John Hancock.

Over the years it has had many incarnations—firehouse, city hall, courthouse, newspaper office, museum. When Queen Elizabeth II visited Boston during our nation's bicentennial, she chose to address Americans from the balcony of Great Britain's former Town House, a building adorned with the lion and unicorn, symbols of the British Crown. Perhaps she was not aware that the first public reading to the Bostonians of the Declaration of Independence from Great Britain took place from that

Artist's rendering of Benjamin Frankin's birthplace

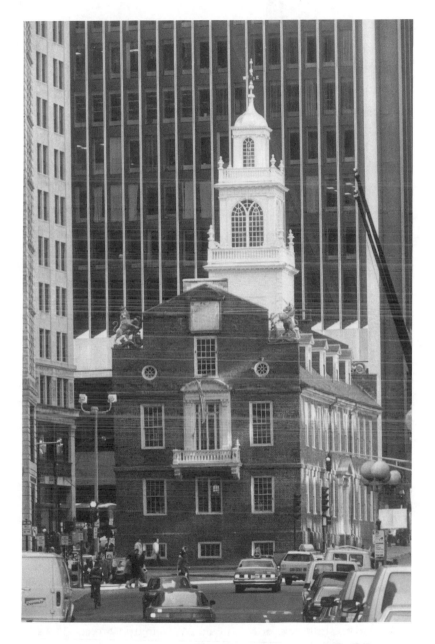

Old State House

Old State House western facade

balcony on July 18, 1776, a custom repeated every July 4 since.

We do not know the name of the architect of this handsome redbrick building, two-and-a half stories high and surmounted by a cupola. We do know that the present structure rose like a phoenix from the ashes of an earlier building.

The original Town House had been the gift of Captain Robert Keayne, an English tailor who became America's first self-made millionaire. The Puritans denounced him for "making too much profit" and forced him to confess publicly his "covetous and corrupt heart."

When Keayne died, however, his will included bequests to shelter "the country people that come with their provisions" and to provide a meeting place for merchants, an armory for the artillery company, a library for the learned, and a chamber for the legislature. Accordingly, the first Town House was erected in 1657 at the intersection of the city's two main thoroughfares, King Street and the Road to the Neck, now State and Washington Streets. It was the middle of an open-air marketplace where all of Boston purchased its food and met to gossip. The Old State House was dedicated to the use of the Massachusetts General Court and the Royal government with its various Courts of Justice. Here the government conducted the business of the province and tried and decided colonial cases.

The colony's business did not, though, run smoothly. Inevitably, the General Court and the Royal government clashed. In 1692 the king, alarmed by a growing independence of spirit in Massachusetts, appointed a Royal Governor to the colony. Still, the colony's representative assembly refused to be ruled. Indeed, by the 1720s the General Court had come to resent the governor's authority to such an extent that it refused to pay his salary. In turn, the governor challenged the powers of the legislature by suspending its privileges. Over the years governors came and governors went, and the representatives of the people of Massachusetts continued their struggle for power.

Occasionally citizens expressed themselves directly. In 1747 a mob, incensed by the Royal Navy's drafting of Americans, marched on the Town House and shattered its windows. To restore order, Governor William Shirley came out on the balcony and delivered a conciliatory speech.

In 1748, flames gutted the Town House, which was quickly rebuilt and restored to its former elegance. Throughout the 1760s liberty's spokesmen used these halls to voice their opposition to British policy. Here John Adams and John Hancock inspired their peers. And here James Otis delivered his impassioned, four-hour speech on the sanctity of individual rights, provoking John Adams to remark, "Then and there, the child Independence was born."

By 1774 the Massachusetts legislature had become a rebel congress, disbanded by the Crown. Members fled British-held Boston and regrouped in Salem. One year later, after the evacuation of the Redcoats from Boston, the Old State House building again became the seat of government, this time the independent government of the Commonwealth of Massachusetts. It was rechristened with a large American eagle adorning its western facade.

Despite its stirring history, the Old State House fell on hard times. In 1881 city fathers were undecided about its utility. Some, on learning that the commercial value of the site was $1.5 million, urged the building's demolition, whereupon the city of Chicago offered to purchase it for reerection on the shores of Lake

41

Michigan. The plan was so inimical to Bostonians that the historic edifice was immediately given a complete restoration.

Today, as the headquarters of the Bostonian Society and its museum, the Old State House retains dignity amid the skyscrapers of the new Boston.

HOURS: *Daily, 9:00 A.M.–5:00 P.M., except Thanksgiving, Christmas, and New Year's Day*
ADMISSION: *Adults, $5.00; senior citizens and students over age eighteen, $4.00; students ages six–eighteen, $1.00; under six, free*
TELEPHONE: *(617) 720–1713*
WEB SITES: *www.bostonhistory.org; www.cityofboston.gov/freedom trail/oldstate.asp*
E-MAIL: *oldstatehouse@bostonhistory.org*
WHEELCHAIR ACCESSIBILITY: *Lift available*

SITE OF THE BOSTON MASSACRE

Congress and State Streets

Beneath the east balcony of the Old State House, a star within a ring of cobblestones marks the site of the first blood shed in the American Revolution.

In October 1768 British troops invaded and occupied Boston. It was a provocative move, escalating the tensions that had come to characterize relations between the Crown and the colony. The Crown had sought to enforce one restrictive act after another, while Bostonians had persistently and sometimes violently defied British authority. Having met with such firm opposition and non-compliance, Royal officials feared an outright insurrection.

In fact, the presence of Redcoats only spurred the Sons of Liberty to greater resistance. For two years the town smoldered, until, in the summer of 1769, the Royal Governor fled to England. Effective regular government came to an end.

By 1770 Bostonians were openly clashing with the Redcoats. Armed conflict seemed inevitable. On the evening of March 5, a band of townsmen goaded two soldiers into a fight, then thrashed them. Fearing reprisal, they sounded the alarm for general action. Bells pealed and people poured into the streets. A crowd gathered

Artist's rendering of the Boston Massacre

in Town House Square in front of the Old State House and surrounded a lone British sentinel.

Soon British troops arrived. The mob turned abusive, waving clubs and threatening bloody murder. People pelted soldiers with snowballs and rocks. They taunted the soldiers, calling out, "come out, you rascals, you bloody-backs, you lobster scoundrels—fire if you dare. God damn you, fire and be damned!"

Scorned and reviled, the soldiers stood in fear for their lives. After one of them was walloped with a stick, he broke down and fired. The rest followed suit, discharging their muskets point-blank at their tormentors.

The mob scattered. But three men lay dead, including Crispus Attucks, the first African American to die for the patriot cause. Of the eight wounded the townsfolk carried away that night, two later died of their injuries. Blood had been shed. The Sons of Liberty had martyrs, and Boston would never be the same.

The countryside erupted. Minutemen prepared to march on Boston and drive the British into the sea. Wholesale slaughter was averted only because Redcoat regiments withdrew to a fort in the harbor and surrendered the soldiers. At the trial, John Adams and Josiah Quincy defended the soldiers. Though all but two were acquitted of manslaughter, the Boston Massacre ever afterward served as a rallying point for the patriot cause.

Every March 5, the event is commemorated with an oration lest Bostonians forget the night "our streets were stained with the Blood of our Brethren, our ears were wounded by the groans of the dying, and our eyes were tormented with the sight of the mangled bodies of the Dead."

President John Adams later declared, "On that night, the foundation of American independence was laid."

WEB SITE: *www.cityofboston.gov/freedomtrail/ bostonmassacre.asp*

FANEUIL HALL

Dock Square

Faneuil Hall once dominated Boston's waterfront. From 1742, when New York–born merchant Peter Faneuil presented his adopted community with the elegant market, until 1825, when Boston filled in the old Town Dock area to meet demands for more market space, the handsome redbrick building welcomed trading ships into a port bustling with business.

But Peter Faneuil was no sober-sided businessman. He had inherited most of his money from his uncle Andrew after promising that he would never marry. He honored the promise and enjoyed a reputation as "the Jolly Bachelor of Boston." He even christened one of his ships *Jolly Bachelor*.

Faneuil proposed a central market building as a remedy for the "disadvantage under which trade was conducted with no market house as a center of exchange." Over the years similar proposals had been defeated. Prosperous shipping merchants, who would benefit from such a facility, supported Faneuil, while peddlers and street hawkers, wary of competition, opposed him. A compromise was reached when authorities allowed Faneuil to build the market at his own expense and to donate it to the city.

To garner greater support for his central market, Faneuil added a second-floor town hall. Ironically, the first major public meeting held in this town hall was a memorial for Peter Faneuil, who died six months after the building was completed. In contrast to the saucy sobriquet of his bachelor days, this son of a French Huguenot refugee was eulogized as "the most public spirited man . . . that ever yet appeared on the northern continent of America."

In the years leading up to the Revolutionary War, the town hall reverberated with tumultuous meetings and midnight assemblies. James Otis, one of the fomenters of the American Revolution, may have dubbed it "Cradle of Liberty." Here Boston's orators thundered their dissent from the Navigation Acts, the Intolerable Acts, and all other acts of the Crown that would restrict the traditional rights and privileges of New England. Here the citizens of the New World claimed the right of free men. Here, too, Sam Adams, the foremost Son of Liberty, led the town meeting to vote its adamant "opposition to Tyrants and their Minions."

Faneuil Hall

Oratory begot direct and sometimes reckless action. One night in 1765 a well-liquored crowd, infuriated by enforcement of the Stamp Act, gathered at Faneuil Hall by the light of a bonfire and attacked the homes of Crown officials. In their frenzy they even tore apart the governor's mansion.

After a fire destroyed the building in 1762, it was quickly rebuilt. In 1805 Charles Bulfinch, the first professional architect in the United States, enlarged and modified the building. Bulfinch doubled the size of the original 40-by-100-foot structure but retained and repeated the Doric and Tuscan pilasters and arched windows of portrait painter John Smibert's original design. He added a spacious third story of his own composition and repositioned the cupola and grasshopper weathervane.

Peter Faneuil himself had chosen the famous gilded grasshopper with the green glass eye to crown his gift to the city. He borrowed the symbol of finance from London, where Martin's Bank and the Royal Exchange were topped by grasshopper vanes. The grasshopper is now so strongly associated with Boston, however, that an American consul once tested citizens claiming to be residents of the city by asking them to identify the most renowned weathervane in the United States.

On November 7, 1960, the eve of the presidential election, John F. Kennedy, ever mindful of historical significance, wound up his campaign with a speech at Faneuil Hall.

Faneuil Hall still serves as a handsome mercantile landmark, but more than that, Faneuil Hall holds a special niche in history and in Boston as a place of public meeting. It is the centerpiece of a scene fully as busy and as colorful as in the days of merchant shipping and revolutionary zeal.

HOURS: *Daily, 9:00* A.M.–*5:00* P.M., *except when a meeting is being held*
ADMISSION: *Free*
TELEPHONE: *(617) 242–5642*
WEB SITE: *www.cityofboston.gov/freedomtrail/faneuilhall.asp*
WHEELCHAIR ACCESSIBILITY: *Elevator*

QUINCY MARKET

Opposite Faneuil Hall

In 1823, one year after Boston became a city, Josiah Quincy, who had served Massachusetts as a congressman in Washington, was elected mayor for the first of what would be five terms.

The dynamic Quincy (1772–1864), later president of Harvard College, greatly improved municipal services. During his tenure he established a standard of service for cities everywhere. He instituted a system for cleaning streets, improved education, and reorganized the police force and fire department. Then he turned his attention to improving and enlarging Boston's limited market facilities "without great expense to the city."

Braving widespread doubt and criticism, the resourceful mayor ordered a landfill of the stagnant waters near the Town Dock. Where wharf rats had scurried, there arose a central marketplace designed by the progressive Boston architect Alexander Parris (1780–1852). The huge two-story building (50 by 535 feet), with its Greek porticoes and domed central pavilion, was constructed in 1825 of granite from the quarries of Quincy, Massachusetts.

The entire project took one year, and sale of the newly created real estate paid for the entire project. Moreover, the brick warehouses that flanked the market and other structures that were built on the six new streets increased the tax base and filled the city's coffers.

Today Quincy Marketplace, redeveloped by James Rouse, constitutes one of the finest urban shopping and dining areas in the world. It serves as an inspiration to old cities everywhere that aspire to revive their downtown areas.

HOURS: *Monday–Saturday, 10:00 A.M.–9:00 P.M.;*
Sunday, noon–6:00 P.M.
ADMISSION: *Free*
TELEPHONE: *(617) 338-2323*
WHEELCHAIR ACCESSIBILITY: *Yes*

Quincy Market

THE TEA PARTY SHIP

Congress Street Bridge; Fort Point Channel

The *Beaver II* is a replica of one of the three British vessels—the others were the *Dartmouth* and the *Eleanor*—that sailed into Boston Harbor in November 1773, carrying cargoes of East India Company tea.

Just the previous month the rebellious colonies had agreed to prevent the British company from docking its ships and selling its tea on American shores. They were determined not to pay the tea tax. Indeed, many colonists had stopped drinking tea altogether rather than pay the tax, the last vestige of the hated Townshend Revenue Bill, which Parliament had enacted in 1767 to tax goods the colonists imported.

The colonists had refused to purchase taxed commodities. Even black mourning clothes ceased to be worn because black wool fabric came from England. This economic boycott so hurt the British that eventually the Townshend taxes were rescinded, save for a small tax on tea. The Crown could not repeal all taxes without appearing to accept the possibility that the colonists were right in their stand of "no taxation without representation."

When the *Eleanor, Dartmouth,* and *Beaver* entered Boston Harbor, the Royal Governor of Massachusetts Bay Colony, Thomas Hutchinson, insisted that they be unloaded and their cargoes sold according to the provisions of the Tea Act. He owned one of the cargoes. The other owners and almost everyone else in Boston hoped that the vessels would simply head back out to sea. Hutchinson, unmoved, double-shotted the cannon at the British fort in the harbor and stationed two warships in the channel.

On December 16 the citizens of Boston held a mass meeting at the Old South Church. While British military leaders focused on the great assembly where Adams and Quincy were haranguing the crowd, another, much smaller meeting was taking place in the back rooms of a printing shop. Availing themselves of a large bowl of potent fishhouse punch, Boston's Sons of Liberty transformed themselves into Mohawk Indians, complete with feathers, blankets, warpaint, and tomahawks. John Adams noted later, however, "They were no ordinary Mohawks."

Artist's rendering of the Boston Tea Party

Early that Saturday evening, just as the meeting at Old South broke up, these "Mohawks" went on the warpath, leading the crowd to the bottom of Pearl Street, where the East India Company shops lay at Griffith's Wharf. With whoops and hollers, eighty or so "braves" clambered aboard the three vessels, broke open tea cases, and flung them into the sea. In less than three hours, they had destroyed all 342 chests of tea. The Redcoats never appeared; the British guns never fired; the ships were not damaged; and no one was hurt. The Tea Party was a resounding success.

The next morning tons of soggy East India Company tea washed ashore. It was the beginning of the end for England in America. Boston and its "Mohawks" had successfully defied the Crown in an act that electrified the colonies and made independence seem possible.

HOURS: *Spring and fall, daily, 9:00* A.M.–*5:00* P.M. *Summer, daily, 9:00* A.M–*6:00* P.M. *Closed Thanksgiving Day and January 1–March 1.* ADMISSION: *Adults, $8.00; seniors and college students with ID, $7.00; ages four–twelve, $4.00; children under four, free*
TELEPHONE: *(617) 338-1773*
WEB SITE: *www.bostonteapartyship.com*
WHEELCHAIR ACCESSIBILITY: *Wheelchairs unable to board*

PAUL REVERE'S HOUSE

19 North Square

Paul Revere's House is the only seventeenth-century wooden dwelling still standing in any major American city. Originally this was the site of the parsonage of the famous Increase Mather, autocratic minister of the first Old North Church and father of his eminent successor, diarist and witch-hunter the Reverend Cotton Mather. The house was about a hundred years old when Revere acquired it, and it was from here that he launched his famous ride to Lexington.

The Mather residence was one of forty-five houses destroyed in the Great Fire of November 18, 1676. Within a year John Jeffs, a mariner, built another house on the site, which he sold in 1681 to

Paul Revere's House

merchant Robert Howard. The new house, typical of seventeenth-century Massachusetts architecture, was built in the English medieval style of the period, with a steep pitch roof; a front overhang, and at the attic level, a gable overhang, both with ornamental drops; small casement windows with diamond-shaped panes; and a simple floor plan that included a massive end chimney.

By contemporary standards the house was unusually spacious, having two large rooms in the front and two more in an ell that extended back toward the garden. The whole structure was framed in heavy carved timbers held together by ingenious joinery and wooden pegs.

Here Robert Howard and his successors dwelled 1 block from the sea, overlooking triangular North Square with its market, guardhouse, meetinghouse, and pump—a veritable beehive of industry and information and one of the town's most fashionable neighborhoods.

It was still a prime location in 1770, when Paul Revere purchased the Howard house for £213⅓ with a mortgage of £160, and moved in with his large family.

Revere, the son of a Huguenot, a Protestant refugee from France named Apollos Rivoire, was the talented possessor of a wide variety of skills and of industry enough to make good use of them. The proprietor of a Hancock's Wharf shop in which he fashioned objects of gold and silver, Revere was also a designer/engraver of copperplate; a manufacturer of false teeth; the owner of a bell foundry and copperworks; the designer, engraver, and printer of the Commonwealth's paper money; a Son of Liberty and prominent rebel organizer; and an excellent horseman who rode as official courier of the Second Continental Congress. He also turned his hand to architecture and added a third story to the old house. In the age before specialization, he was Boston's preeminent generalist.

Today Revere is remembered for his midnight ride rather than for his bills and bells and bowls. The galloping rhythms and stirring language of Henry Wadsworth Longfellow's ballad, published in 1863, made Paul Revere one of the most celebrated heroes of the American Revolution. With the possible exception of "The Night before Christmas," "Paul Revere's Ride" may be the only poem of which every American can recite at least one couplet.

Paul Revere's House

After the Revolution Revere settled down to a life of hard and rewarding work as one of the nation's first industrialists, developing his bell foundry and copperworks, as well as a cannon foundry, into important Boston enterprises.

Revere sold his house in 1800, when he moved to more elegant quarters; but the three-story North Square building remained associated with his memory and was preserved through many years of neighborhood demolition and renewal.

The Paul Revere Memorial Association acquired the house in 1907 and, during the next two years, sheared off the third story and restored the building to its probable 1676 appearance. Today it is a showcase for some beautiful old furniture and china (not much of it is Revere's), two enormous fireplaces with brick ovens and antique utensils, portions of 1750 wallpaper depicting in block pattern the Church of Saint Mary le Bow in London, and an assortment of Revere's etchings and manuscript letters. Except for the Revere memorabilia, its most famous owner might have difficulty recognizing his residence, but John Jeffs, Robert Howard, and even Increase Mather would feel right at home.

HOURS: *April 15–October 31, daily, 9:30* A.M.*–5:15* P.M.;
November 1–April 14, 9:30 A.M.*–4:15* P.M.;
closed Mondays, January through March;
closed Thanksgiving, Christmas, and New Year's Day
ADMISSION: *Adults, $2.50; seniors and students, $2.00;*
ages five–seventeen, $1.00; children under five, free
TELEPHONE: *(617) 523-2338*
WEB SITES: *www.paulreverehouse.org; www.cityofboston.gov/*
paulrevere.asp
WHEELCHAIR ACCESSIBILITY: *First floor and program area*

SAINT STEPHEN'S CHURCH

Hanover Street, Facing the Prado

Saint Stephen's Church is the only house of worship designed by
Charles Bulfinch that is still standing in Boston. The church features
a pilastered facade in what is described as a "bold and commanding
style," surmounted by a clock tower, a belfry, and an Eastern dome.
Bulfinch relieved the front elevation with a Palladian window, a
lunette above, and his characteristic graceful blind-arch windows.

Bulfinch's church cost $26,570 to build. The cornerstone was
laid on September 23, 1802, and the building dedicated on May
2, 1804. The following year the congregation purchased a bell for
$800 from the foundry of Paul Revere. And in 1830 the church
acquired an organ made by William Marcellus Goodrich, the
leading organ maker in America.

The congregation already had a long history before it acquired
the building. In 1714 seventeen successful Boston artisans had
banded together to form a religious society that, they said, would
provide spiritual sustenance to the city's "humble" citizens. "Unas-
sisted by the more wealthy part of the community except by their
prayers and good wishes," the artisans erected the New North
Church building, a small wooden meetinghouse.

Under the Reverend John Webb, the society prospered. But in
1719, with the introduction of the Reverend Peter Thatcher as
Webb's colleague, a bitter and messy division developed within the
group. As a result, a minority broke away to found the New Brick
North Church. They topped their new house of worship with the

Saint Stephen's Church

city's first weathercock. According to local legend, the weathervane was barely installed on its perch when a gust of wind turned the cockerel's head in the direction of New North. A bystander, aware that the cock is a symbol of the Apostle Peter's denial and that Reverend Thatcher's first name was Peter, derisively crowed three times in the direction of New North. The New Brick was therefore also called "Revenge Church" and the "Cockerel Church." After the New Brick North Church was razed in 1871, the weathervane found a perch on the spire of First Church in Cambridge, Congregational, where it can be seen today.

In 1730 New North was enlarged. The congregation continued to grow and after the Revolution required a larger home. Down came the old wooden New North, and in its place rose a new brick New North (not to be confused with the New Brick North Church), using some of the old building's timbers.

Like many other congregations in the early part of the nineteenth century, New North's adopted Unitarianism. As early as the 1820s, however, the North End was changing, and by the 1850s the area had become solidly Irish Catholic. The Catholic Church acquired the building in 1862. The Bulfinch cupola was changed, and, to accommodate the widening of Hanover Street in 1870, Saint Stephen's was moved back 16 feet and raised 6 inches on its foundation.

Rose Fitzgerald, mother of President John F. Kennedy, was christened at Saint Stephen's in 1890. By 1900, however, the Irish of the North End were replaced by the Italians, whose descendants continue to worship here.

In 1964 Boston's Richard Cardinal Cushing authorized a complete restoration of Saint Stephen's, including restoring the cupola and lowering the building to its original foundation height. In the course of this project, workmen discovered the original side-entrance doors, bricked up, with hardware intact. Now Bulfinch's church once again looks much as he intended.

HOURS: *Open daily at 7:30* A.M.*; Mass is held Sunday at 8:30 and 11:00* A.M.*; Monday at 5:15* P.M.*; Tuesday–Friday at 7:30* A.M.*; Saturday at 5:15* P.M.
ADMISSION: *Free*
TELEPHONE: *(617) 523–1230*
WHEELCHAIR ACCESSIBILITY: *No*

PAUL REVERE MALL

Hanover Street, Next to the Old North Church

Paul Revere Mall, the small park linking Christ Church ("Old North") and Saint Stephen's Church, is dominated by Cyrus Dallin's equestrian statue of that celebrated midnight rider, Paul Revere. Thirteen bronze plaques set in the Prado walls recount the role that the North End and its people played in the history of Boston from 1630 to 1918.

The North End's most famous resident by far, Paul Revere rode from Boston to Lexington on April 18, 1775, to bring the latest intelligence about the British to John Hancock and Sam Adams. General Thomas Gage and his troops were preparing to march out and capture the colonial militia's contraband muskets, gunpowder, and cannons stored in Concord. No one knew, however, when the British would march or the route they would take.

On the evening of April 18, 1775, Redcoats began to gather on Boston Common. It soon became apparent that their destination was Lexington and Concord. At about eleven o'clock that evening, the light of two lanterns shone from the steeple of Christ Church. This was Revere's prearranged signal to the patriots in Charlestown that the British would be advancing from Boston by a water route to the Charlestown shore, and then to Concord. Revere wrapped himself in a heavy cloak, slipped down to the waterfront, and "with muffled oar, silently rowed to the Charlestown shore," safely passing by the illuminated man-o'-war *Somerset*. Just as the moonlight revealed British transport barges rounding the point, Revere docked quietly and mounted Deacon Larkin's sturdy horse.

The rest is history, or poetry. Revere rode off through Cambridge to Medford, and from Medford to Lexington, calling, "The British are coming." He thundered past sleeping farms, dismounting and pounding on doors at every village common or knot of country homes. Behind him, he left bells ringing and men shouting and dogs barking. Minutemen poured out of their homes to form ranks against the enemy. Other horsemen saddled up and rode off to spread the word. By the time Revere reached Lexington, the whole countryside was up in arms.

Before dawn Revere was captured on his way back from Concord by an advance party of British cavalry. They detained him

*Paul Revere statue with the steeple of the
Old North Church in the background*

until their troops had marched past on the way to Lexington Common. His captors had no way of knowing that the Yankee horseman they held had ruined their plans. For before the sun went down that day, the militia of Massachusetts gave His Majesty's troops a terrible beating. It was the first day of the Revolutionary War.

OLD NORTH CHURCH

193 Salem Street

The building we know today as Old North Church, also called Christ Church, was erected in 1723; it is the oldest house of worship still standing in Boston. The second Episcopal church in Boston—the first is King's Chapel—it was designed by the Boston print-seller William Price in the manner of Sir Christopher Wren's London churches. The original brick tower was surmounted by one of the architectural wonders of old Boston, a magnificent spire soaring 191 feet above the street.

Old North Church, once a bastion of Loyalist support for the British Empire, may be the best-known landmark of the Revolutionary era. Thanks to Henry Wadsworth Longfellow's poem "The Landlord's Tale: Paul Revere's Ride," every schoolchild in America learns that Revere's ride was triggered by a lantern signal: "One if by land, and two if by sea."

The church sexton, Robert Newman, was a friend of Revere and shone the lanterns on the night of April 18, 1775, thus alerting the Charlestown rebels of the British intention to cross over to their shore. Revere himself, as he rowed out on the flood tide, must have seen the double light shining out from Christ Church. Before he even touched shore, the secret English invasion was common knowledge, the march on Concord revealed. (One of the lanterns spied by Paul Revere is on display at the Concord Museum.)

When the British General Thomas Gage, who attended services at Christ Church (pew 62), chose the steeple as a vantage point from which to observe the burning of Charlestown and the British disaster at Bunker Hill, he probably did not know of the church's role in warning the patriots. The British leader of the Lexington–Concord expedition, Major John Pitcairn, died heroically at Bunker Hill and is said to be buried in a vault below the church.

The historic steeple of Longfellow's poem—the gift of a group of merchants from British Honduras who in return received the use of a handsome box pew—came crashing down in the Great Gale of 1804. The steeple fell on an old tenement house, which was destroyed, but fortunately no one was injured. Charles Bulfinch, carefully preserving its "symmetry and proportions," provided a new design with a steeple that was 16 feet shorter. The Bulfinch steeple fell victim to a hurricane in 1954. The present steeple, a reproduction of the first, is capped with Shem Drowne's original 1740 weathervane, a banner with a ball and star above.

In 1744 Dr. Timothy Cutler, the spiritual leader of the congregation of wealthy and influential families, most of whom were connected with the Royal government of the province, sailed to Britain to obtain the chief ornament of the church: a marvelous chime of eight bells inscribed with such sentiments as "We are the first ring of bells cast for the British Empire in North America," "Since generosity has opened our mouths, our tongues shall ring aloud its praise," and, of course, "God preserve the Church of England." The carillon—young Paul Revere was one of the early bell ringers—still rings out with extraordinary beauty on Sundays after 11:00 A.M. service, on the Fourth of July, and for every major historical occasion, including presidential inaugurations.

Many of the church's interior fittings were donated by philanthropic Englishmen interested in propagating the doctrines of the Church of England in Puritan Boston. King George II himself donated the silver communion service. Captain Thomas Gruchy, commander of the privateer *Queen of Hungary*, presented the four trumpeting angels that grace the choir loft, booty from a French vessel.

Also of interest is the so-called Vinegar Bible, on view in a case in the museum next door. Printed in 1717 by John Baskett, it contains a misprint. The twentieth chapter of Saint Luke, at the top of the first column of the page, reads "The parable of the vinegar" instead of "The parable of the vineyard."

After more than two centuries, Old North Church is still an active Episcopal congregation, with services on Sunday mornings. Brass plates on the pews bear names of Revolutionary-era families, many of whose descendants still worship here, including those of

Old North Church

Paul Revere (pew 54). The bust of George Washington at the front of the church is a fine likeness of the president, according to the Marquis de Lafayette.

On April 18, 1975, President Gerald Ford inaugurated the nation's bicentennial year at this church, and on July 11, 1976, Prince Philip accompanied Queen Elizabeth, the first reigning British monarch ever to set foot in Boston, when she made Old North Church her first stop in the city.

Incidentally, this is not Boston's first Old North Church. The *old* Old North Church, built in 1650 in North Square, was destroyed by fire in 1676, was rebuilt, and stood for another hundred years before the British tore it down for firewood.

HOURS: *Visitors are welcome daily, 9:00 A.M.–5:00 P.M. Sunday services are held at 9:00 A.M., 11:00 A.M., and 5:00 P.M. Open every day 9:00 A.M.–6:00 P.M. for prayer and meditation.*

ADMISSION: *Free, but a donation is suggested.*

TELEPHONE: *(617) 523–6676*

WEB SITES: *www.oldnorth.com; www.cityofboston.gov/ freedomtrail/oldnorth.asp*

WHEELCHAIR ACCESSIBILITY: *Yes*

TALES OF A WAYSIDE INN

THE LANDLORD'S TALE:
Paul Revere's Ride

Listen, my children, and you shall hear
of the midnight ride of Paul Revere,
On the eighteenth of April, in Seventy-five;
Hardly a man is now alive
Who remembers that famous day and year.

He said to his friend, "If the British march
By land or sea from the town to-night,
Hang a lantern aloft in the belfry arch
Of the North Church tower as a signal light,—
One, if by land, and two if by sea;
And I on the opposite shore will be,
Ready to ride and spread the alarm
Through every Middlesex village and farm,
For the country folk to be up and to arm."

Then he said, "Good-night" and with muffled oar
Silently row'd to the Charlestown shore,
Just as the moon rose over the bay,
Where swinging wide at her moorings lay
The Somerset, British man-of-war;
A phantom ship, with each mast and spar
Across the moon like a prison bar,
And a huge black hulk, that was magnified
By its own reflection in the tide.

Meanwhile, his friend, through alley and street,
Wanders and watches with eager ears,
Till in the silence around him he hears
The muster of men at the Barrack-door,
The sound of arms, and the tramp of feet,
And the measured tread of the grenadiers
Marching down to their boats on the shore.

Then he climb's the tower of the Old North Church,
By the wooden stairs, with stealthy tread,
To the belfry-chamber overhead,
And startled the pigeons from their perch
On the sombre rafters, that found him made
Masses and moving shapes of shade—
By the trembling ladder, steep and tall,
To the highest window in the wall,
Where he paused to listen and look down
A moment on the roofs of the town.
And the moonlight flowing over all.

Beneath, in the churchyard, lay the dead,
In their night-encampment on the hill,
Wrapp'd in silence so deep and still
That he could hear, like a sentinel's tread,
The watchful night-wind, as it went
Creeping along from tent to tent,
And seeming to whisper, "All is well!"
A moment only he feels the spell
Of the place and the hour, and the secret dread
Of the lonely belfry and the dead;
For suddenly all his thoughts are bent
On a shadowy something far away,
Where the river widens to meet the bay,—
a line of black that bends and floats
On the rising tide like a bridge of boats.

Meanwhile, impatient to mount and ride,
Booted and spurr'd, with a heavy stride
On the opposite shore walk'd Paul Revere.
Now he patted his horse's side,
Now he gazed at the landscape far and near,
Then, impetuous, stamp'd the earth,
And turn'd and tighten'd his saddle-girth;
But mostly he watch'd with eager search
The belfry-tower of Old North Church,
As it rose above the graves on the hill,
Lonely and spectral and sombre and still.
An lo! as he looks, on the belfry's height
A glimmer, and then a gleam of light!

He springs to the saddle, the bridle he turns,
But lingers and gazes, till full on his sight
A second lamp in the belfry burns.

A hurry of hoofs in a village street,
A shape in the moonlight, a bulk in the dark,
And beneath, from the pebbles, in passing a spark
Struck out by a steed flying fearless and fleet:
That was all; and yet, through the gloom and the light,
The fate of a nation was riding that night;
And the spark struck out by the steed, in his flight,
Kindled the land into flame with its heat.

He has left the village and mounted the steep,
And beneath him, tranquil and broad and deep,
Is the Mystic, meeting the ocean tides,
And under the alders that skirt its edge,
Now soft on the sand, now loud on the ledge,
Is heard the tramp of his steed as he rides.

It was twelve by the village clock
When he cross'd the bridge into Medford town.
He heard the crowing of the cock,
And the barking of the farmer's dog,
And felt the damp of the river fog,
That rises after the sun goes down.

It was one by the village clock
When he galloped into Lexington.
He saw the gilded weathercock
Swim in the moonlight as he pass'd,
And the meeting-house windows, blank and bare,
Gaze at him with spectral glare,
As if they already stood aghast
At the bloody work they would look upon.

It was two by the village clock
When he came to the bridge in Concord town.
He heard the bleating of the flock,
And the twitter of birds among the trees,
And felt the breath of the morning breeze

Blowing over the meadows brown.
And one was safe and asleep in his bed
Who at the bridge would be first to fall,
Who that day would be lying dead,
Pierced by a British musket-ball.

You know the rest; in the books you have read,
How the British regulars fired and fled,—
How the farmers gave them ball for ball,
From behind each fence and farmyard wall,
Chasing the red-coats down the lane,
Then crossing the fields to emerge again
Under the trees at the turn of the road,
And only pausing to fire and load.
So through the night rode Paul Revere,
And so through the night went his cry of alarm
To every Middlesex village and farm,—
A cry of defiance and not of fear,
A voice in the darkness, a knock at the door,
And a word that shall echo for evermore!
For, borne on the night-wind of the Past,
Through all our history, to the last,
In the hour of darkness, and peril, and need,
The people will waken and listen to hear
The hurrying hoof-beats of that steed,
And the midnight message of Paul Revere.

—HENRY WADSWORTH LONGFELLOW, 1863

COPP'S HILL

Hull and Snowhill Streets

Copp's Hill Burial Ground in the North End, Boston's second-oldest cemetery, comprises three or four graveyards of different periods. The oldest, in the northeasterly section bounded by Charter and Snowhill Streets, dates from 1660.

The area near Snowhill Street was reserved for slave burials, although the tall black monument near the Snowhill Street fence is a memorial to Prince Hall, a freed slave and leader of Boston's free black community. He helped sponsor Boston's first school for black children and founded the African Grand Lodge of Massachusetts, the world's first black Masonic lodge. About 1,000 free blacks are also buried here. Most were residents of New Guinea, a pre-Revolutionary community at the foot of the hill.

Although many of Copp's Hill's old stones are gone, appropriated years ago by North Enders for chimneys and doorsteps, the heraldic markers set in the west wall remain, and the cemetery is filled with wonderful epitaphs and tombstones with quaint inscriptions.

Here lie the mortal remains of Messrs. Milk and Beer and of Mistresses Brown, Scarlet, and White. Close by are the stones of Samuel Mower and Theodocia Hay. The illustrious Mathers, for several generations the theological dictators of Boston, are interred in their family tomb. And Edmund Hartt, builder of the USS *Constitution*, rests within cannonshot of his creation. Robert Newman, the sexton who signaled Paul Revere with two lanterns hung in the steeple of Old North Church, is buried here, too.

In the early 1600s a fort occupied the hill, which has also been known as Snow Hill, Mill Field, and Windmill Hill. Boston's first windmill was acquired in August 1632 from Cambridge, where it failed to grind except with a westerly wind. Atop this hill it successfully caught ocean breezes to grind corn for the city's early settlers.

The Old North Burying Ground was set aside in 1659 for North End residents. It is now named for William Copp, a shoemaker who settled in the North End after emigrating from Stratford-on-Avon, England. He owned the land before selling it to the town for a cemetery and is buried here, too.

By the time of the Revolution, several shipyards and wharves had been established at the base of Copp's Hill. Its crest

69

Copp's Hill

commanded an excellent view of Boston and, across the Charles River, of Charlestown. Here in June 1775 the British set up a battery that bombarded Charlestown during the Battle of Bunker Hill and set that town ablaze. Generals John Burgoyne and Henry Clinton used Copp's Hill as a command post during the battle and were witness to the doubly grisly sight of an entire town burning to the ground and, just beyond, an army of British regulars falling dead or wounded.

Many gravestones bear the pockmarks of musket balls. The chipped stone of Captain Daniel Malcolm, "A True Son of Liberty . . . an enemy to Oppression," bears testimony to the pleasure of British troops in using it for target practice.

Like Beacon Hill, Copp's Hill was once a good deal higher. It presented an almost sheer cliff to the water side, sloping gradually back toward the town as a three-acre field. The crest of the hill was removed in 1807 for use as a Mill Pond landfill, where North Station now sits, and the site of both the windmill and the

British battery disappeared into the mud. For more than a decade, the hill was diminished for fill. Yet Copp's Hill endures, an irreducible element of Old Boston.

HOURS: *Spring, summer, and fall, daily,*
9:00 A.M.*–5:00* P.M.*; winter, daily, 9:00* A.M.*–3:00* P.M.
ADMISSION: *Free*

TELEPHONE: *(617) 635-7389*
WEB SITES: *www.nps.gov/bost/1Copps_Hill.htm;*
www.cityofboston.gov/freedomtrail/coppshill.asp
WHEELCHAIR ACCESSIBILITY: *No*

USS CONSTITUTION

Charlestown Navy Yard

The USS *Constitution,* launched on October 12, 1797, is the oldest commissioned warship afloat in the world.

After the American Revolution, the American Navy was disbanded, and for more than a decade no warships sailed under the Stars and Stripes. By 1793, however, the Barbary pirates of North Africa were preying on U.S. merchant vessels, demanding tribute and ransom, so in March 1794 President George Washington approved an act to build six ships for the defense of the nation.

During the summer of 1795, Edmund Hartt laid the white oak keel of a frigate, built to carry forty-four guns, at his North End shipyard. Although peace was made that fall with the ruler of Algiers, work continued for two years on the Constitution. Its timbers were white oak from New Jersey, New Hampshire, and Massachusetts; live oak from Saint Simons Island of Georgia; and yellow pine from Georgia and the Carolinas. Its white pine masts came from Maine; its copper bolts and spikes, from Paul Revere's foundry.

Two hundred four feet from stem to stern and 44 feet broad, the vessel carried fifty-four guns and 450 men. It displaced 2,200 tons and could carry provisions for a crew of 475. Its mainmast towered 189 feet into the sky, and its sails, comprising nearly an acre of canvas, were constructed at the Old Granary, the only building large enough to accommodate the work. The Skillings brothers carved the original figurehead of Hercules presenting a scroll, symbolic of the Constitution of the United States.

USS Constitution

By July 1798, the United States had become involved in an undeclared war with France, and the *Constitution* was sent on patrol in the West Indies until a settlement could be reached.

In 1803 the *Constitution* was the flagship of a squadron sent to attack the persistent corsairs of Tripoli. Under Commodore Edward Preble the frigate pounded Tripoli into submission. In the end, the governor of Tripoli came aboard to initial a draft of the peace treaty.

The United States wished to remain neutral in the war that had broken out between France and Great Britain in 1803, but after years of increasing British harassment of American shipping, Congress declared war on England in June 1812. A British journalist voiced his country's scornful attitude toward the action, writing that "fir-built" American frigates "manned by a handful of bastards and outlaws" were no match for the British Navy.

Nevertheless, on August 19, 1812, under Captain Isaac Hull the Constitution achieved what historians cite as "probably the most brilliant American victory of the war." She engaged the forty-nine-gun British frigate *Guerriere* off Nova Scotia and within an hour reduced the ship to a hulk. Having watched enemy cannonballs bounce off the *Constitution*'s sturdy hull, crewmen celebrated their ship's first naval victory, dubbing her "Old Ironsides."

Under a new captain, William Bainbridge, the *Constitution* continued its record of outstanding service. On December 29, 1812, off the coast of Brazil, after a spirited and terrible exchange of broadsides, the forty-seven-gun frigate *Java* was demasted and her commander fatally wounded. A lieutenant ordered the colors struck, and the British frigate was blown up.

Two years later, under Captain Charles Stewart, the intrepid *Constitution* engaged the British warships *Cyane* and *Levant* off the coast of Portugal. With skillful maneuvering and deadly cannonfire, "Old Ironsides" soon made a wreck of the *Cyane*. The *Levant* fought on and nearly escaped but returned to battle and fell prey to the larger American vessel.

Thus ended the illustrious fighting career of the USS *Constitution:* in forty battles never beaten and never boarded.

The warship retired to Boston, where it remained until 1821, when it cruised the Mediterranean. It returned in 1828 to rumors that the U.S. Navy had decided to scrap it, and in 1830, condemned as unseaworthy, the *Constitution* was ordered destroyed. A student at Harvard, Oliver Wendell Holmes, responded with a poem of protest. His verse provoked such an outcry that Congress appropriated funds to restore the frigate.

By 1897, one hundred years after her maiden voyage, the ship was rotting away. In his campaign to save the vessel, John F. Fitzgerald, maternal grandfather of President John F. Kennedy, spoke before Congress and presented a resolution to preserve the frigate as a memorial. Congress authorized repairs so minimal, however, that in 1905 the historic ship was again headed for destruction, this time as a training target for the fleet.

Americans protested, and Congress appropriated $100,000 for additional repairs. For the next twenty years, the ship remained at her pier in Boston as a museum but continued to decay. Congress had little enthusiasm for preserving the *Constitution*, enacting a bill in 1925 that authorized reconstruction but provided no funds for the work. After a public fund-raising campaign—even schoolchildren answered the call by donating their pennies—the collected sum still fell short of what was needed. Finally, Congress appropriated money to complete the work.

Totally overhauled, the *Constitution* departed Boston on July 2, 1931, on one of the longest voyages of its career—more than three years and ninety-one ports—greeted everywhere by admiring crowds. Afterwards, it returned to its home port, where for more than fifty years, it has served as flagship for Commandants of the First Naval District.

Now the *Constitution* is berthed at the Charlestown Navy Yard, next to its newer neighbor, the World War II destroyer USS *Cassin Young*. Once a year, "Old Ironsides" sails into Boston Harbor for a turnaround cruise, honored with a cortege of streaming fireboats.

HOURS: *Daily, including Sundays and holidays,*
10:00 A.M.–*4:00* P.M.
ADMISSION: *Free*
TELEPHONE: *(617) 242–5670 or 242–5671*
WEB SITE: *www.ussconstitution.navy.mil*
WHEELCHAIR ACCESSIBILITY: *Yes*
CONSTITUTION MUSEUM HOURS: *Daily, 9:00* A.M.–*6:00* P.M.,
May 1 through October 15; daily, 10:00 A.M.–*5:00* P.M., *October 16*
through April 30. Closed Thanksgiving, Christmas, and
New Year's Day.
TELEPHONE: *(617) 426–1812*
WEB SITE: *www.ussconstitutionmuseum.org*

"Old Ironsides"

Old Ironsides

Ay, tear her tattered ensign down!
Long has it waved on high,
And many an eye had danced to see
That banner in the sky:
Beneath it rung the battle shout,
And burst the cannon's roar—
The meteor of the ocean air
Shall sweep the clouds no more.

Her decks, once red with heroes' blood,
Where knelt the vanquished foe,
When winds were hurrying o'er the flood,
And waves were white below.
No more shall feel the victor's tread,
Or know the conquered knee—
The harpies of the shore shall pluck
the eagle of the sea!

Oh, better that her shattered hulk
Should sink beneath the wave;
Her thunders shook the mighty deep,
And there should be her grave;
Nail to the mast her holy flag,
Set every threadbare sail,
And give her to the god of storms,
The lightning and the gale!

—OLIVER WENDELL HOLMES, 1830

BUNKER HILL

Charlestown

The British and the colonists both made so many mistakes that some historians call the Battle of Bunker Hill the "Battle of Blunders."

Not only did the colonists fortify the wrong hill, Breed's Hill, but they also dug themselves into a trap with a narrow escape. The

British, on the other hand, so disdained their ragtag opponents that they ignored good military strategy. Instead of closing the trap, they routed the citizen soldiers, and the majority escaped.

Providing protective cover for the retreating colonials, however, cost the life of the much-loved Dr. Joseph Warren. The physician had served as president of the provincial congress and chairman of the Massachusetts Committee on Safety, an interim government the colony established after the Royal Governor departed.

Fought on June 17, 1775, the first major battle of the Revolutionary War was also the bloodiest. More than 1,400 men, mostly British soldiers, died in an hour and a half. The British General Thomas Gage noted, "The rebels are not the despicable rabble too many have supposed."

Still, the colonials lost the battle. But it was not for lack of courage. One of at least six black soldiers, twenty-eight-year-old Salem Poor, who went on to fight with George Washington at Valley Forge, was honored with a 1976 bicentennial postage stamp as a "gallant soldier." Notwithstanding the patriots' defeat, Charlestown observes the battle's anniversary with pomp and parades every June 17.

As for the famous Quincy granite monument, it almost didn't get off the ground. On June 17, 1825, the fiftieth anniversary of the battle, the cornerstone was laid with great fanfare. Trowel in hand, the Marquis de Lafayette, the nation's guest, spread the mortar. Two hundred veterans of the Revolutionary War, including forty who had fought in the celebrated engagement, looked on. Daniel Webster, the rousing orator, proclaimed, "The consequences of the Battle of Bunker Hill are greater than those of any ordinary conflict."

But the venture, which had begun so optimistically, experienced setbacks. The foundation proved inadequate; the cornerstone was quietly relocated. Construction started anew, but the tower was barely 40 feet high when money ran out. The architect and builder, Solomon Willard, donated his services as a "patriotic duty." The project, however, was abandoned, $23,000 in debt.

Another attempt to complete the monument began in 1834. About 45 feet were added before work was again halted for lack of funds. The memorial, undertaken with high hopes, became a public joke. Neighbors proposed to tear down the eyesore. It probably would have been razed, had not a feisty lady from Maine stepped in.

Bunker Hill Monument

When she arrived in Boston in 1828, Sarah Josepha Hale, the fervently patriotic daughter of a Revolutionary War officer, was a recent widow and the sole support of five young children. Her imagination and emotions were immediately engaged by the drive to erect the monument, and she began writing editorials favorable to the endeavor in the *Ladies' Magazine*, precursor of *Godey's Lady's Book*. Then she took the unprecedented step of conducting a public fund-raising drive.

At first, members of the Monument Association, all men, refused to cooperate with Widow Hale. Finally, they accepted her help on condition that the "efforts of the ladies will not degrade the character of men."

With the publication of her patriotic poem "The Last of the Band," Hale raised the first $3,000 of the $100,000 required to complete the monument. Then she rented Quincy Hall, the largest exposition space in Boston, for a fair.

Throughout the summer of 1840, New England women and women from as far away as Ohio and the Carolinas busily sewed, embroidered, prepared straw work, beaded, quilted, did waxwork, put up jellies and pickles, and produced whatever their hands could contrive. When the fair opened on September 8, more than 4,000 people attended. Seven days later it closed, and after all expenses had been paid out, the women's earnings exceeded $30,000. In the Monument Association report, the men acknowledged that the sum was "beyond expectations."

The effort was now supported by newspapers throughout New England; donations poured in. When the fund was $20,000 short, Amos Lawrence, a Boston merchant, pledged $10,000 if someone else would match it. Judah Touro, the orphaned son of the rabbi of a synagogue in Newport, Rhode Island, had as a youth been taken in by an aunt in Boston. Now a successful entrepreneur, he donated the money to top off the 221-foot, 294-step granite obelisk. He had wished to remain anonymous, but on June 17, 1843, at the monument's dedication ceremonies, attended by President John Tyler and his entire cabinet, the two benefactors were acknowledged.

Amos and Judah, venerated names;
Patriarch and Prophet press their equal claim.
Christian and Jew, they carry out one plan,
For though of different faith,
Each is in heart a man.

At last the first monument built through public donation was completed. Sarah Josepha Hale is credited with organizing the first women's auxiliary, a model for women's clubs that helped men achieve their goals. Bunker Hill Monument is generally considered the first publicized tourist attraction and the first historic site in America to be restored.

HOURS: *Daily, 9:00* A.M.*–4:30* P.M.
Lodge with displays open until 5:00 P.M.
Closed Thanksgiving, Christmas, and
New Year's Day.
ADMISSION: *Free*
TELEPHONE: *(617) 242-5641*
WEB SITE: *www.cityofboston.gov/freedomtrail/bunkerhill.asp*
WHEELCHAIR ACCESSIBILITY: *Rest rooms and lodge*

INDEX

ABOUT THE EDITOR

Erica Bollerud lives in Medford, Massachusetts. She follows the
Freedom Trail every morning to her job at the State House, where
she works as a legislative aid to State Senator Robert O'Leary.